The Big Volley
Coloring Book

An Amazing Volleyball Coloring Book
For Teens and Adults

By
Debbie Russell

**Hello friends! Thank you from the bottom of my families heart
for buying one of my coloring books!
IF YOU ENJOYED MY BOOK, PLEASE LEAVE A REVIEW!
I AM AN INDEPENDANT AUTHOR & ILLUSTRATOR. POSITIVE
REVIEWS HELP OTHERS TO FIND MY BOOKS ONLINE!**

COMPLEXITY: When my mom Ethlyn was facing cancer and going through chemotherapy, she renewed her interest in coloring. I was frustrated by trying to find her coloring books that had different levels of complexity. I design my books for a variety of coloring enthusiasts.

-A third of the designs are complex,
-A third of the designs are medium complexity.
-A third of the designs are simpler for when you want to color but you have less time and don't want an overwhelming project to complete.

BLOTTING PAGES: AT the end of the book you will find blotting pages. When self-publishing, Independent authors are not given a choice of paper thickness nor given the option of perforating the pages for easy Removal. Possibly in the future, the printers will let us have those Features because we know how important they are.

The blotting pages should help you to be able to use markers if you so desire without ruining the pages underneath. Simply remove one and slip it underneath the design.

You can also use the pages to test and keep track of your color choices.

Compendium Of Included Designs

Compendium Of Included Designs

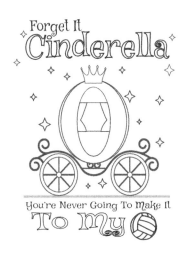

Compendium Of Included Designs

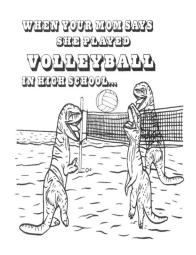

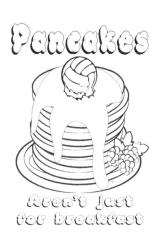

Compendium Of Included Designs

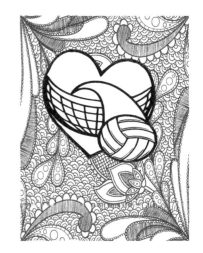

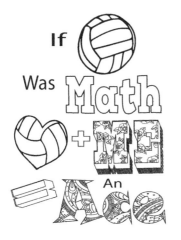

Compendium Of Included Designs

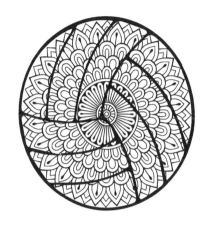

Compendium Of Included Designs

Compendium Of Included Designs

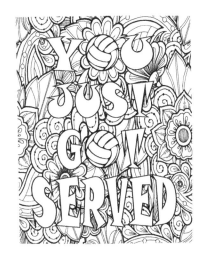

Turn...

Sweat Into

STRENGTH

Fear Into

COURAGE

Doubt Into

BELIEF

Practice Into

VICTORY

Forget It Cinderella

You're Never Going To Make It

To My 🏐

Pancakes

Aren't just for breakfast

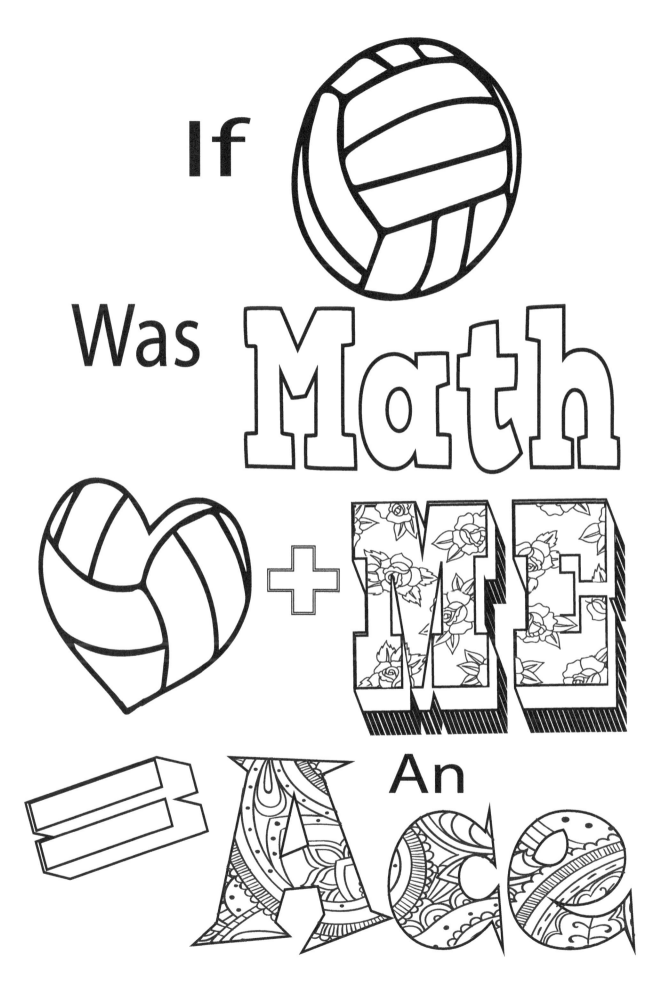

Setters are Better

WHEN YOU MAKE AN
AMAZING SAVE

AND YOUR TEAM
JUST LETS IT DROP

BLOTTING PAGE

Use This Page To Prevent Marker Bleed Through. Or To Test And Keep Track Of Your Color Selections So You Can Pick Just The Right Colors Or Not Forget Which Ones You Were Using.

BLOTTING PAGE

Use This Page To Prevent Marker Bleed Through. Or To Test
And Keep Track Of Your Color Selections So You Can Pick
Just The Right Colors Or Not Forget Which Ones You Were Using.

Made in the USA
Middletown, DE
06 October 2022

12165505R00051